DARK WATER SONGS

ALSO BY MARY LOU SOUTAR-HYNES

Travelling Light
The Fires of Naming

DARK WATER SONGS

poems

Mary Lou Soutar-Hynes

inanna poetry & fiction series

Inanna Publications and Education Inc.
Toronto, Canada

Copyright © 2013 Mary Lou Soutar-Hynes

Except for the use of short passages for review purposes, no part of this book may be reproduced, in part or in whole, or transmitted in any form or by any means, electronically or mechanically, including photocopying, recording, or any information or storage retrieval system, without prior permission in writing from the publisher.

Canada Council for the Arts   Conseil des Arts du Canada   ONTARIO ARTS COUNCIL CONSEIL DES ARTS DE L'ONTARIO

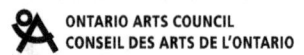

The publisher gratefully acknowledges the support of the Canada Council for the Arts and the Ontario Arts Council for its publishing program.

The publisher is also grateful for the kind support received from an Anonymous Fund at The Calgary Foundation.

Front cover artwork: John Oughton, "Casino Night"

Library and Archives Canada Cataloguing in Publication

Soutar-Hynes, Mary Lou
     Dark water songs : poems / Mary Lou Soutar-Hynes.

(Inanna poetry & fiction series)
ISBN 978-1-926708-94-2

     I. Title. II. Series: Inanna poetry and fiction series

PS8587.O9756D37 2013   C811'.6   C2013-901782-8

Printed and bound in Canada

Inanna Publications and Education Inc.
210 Founders College, York University
4700 Keele Street
Toronto, Ontario, Canada M3J 1P3
Telephone: (416) 736-5356 Fax (416) 736-5765
Website: www.inanna.ca
Email: inanna.publications@inanna.ca

to my sisters

Contents

Pinturas ciegas   1

Section I: In the Manner of Tides

Anatomy of Green   5
By Invitation   6
Notes from the Archipelago   7
     1. *Today*   7
     2. *Here, there are revelations*   8
     3. *Fragments*   9
     4. *A Geography of Voices*   10
     5. *Reefs*   11
Maybe   12
To a Creole Ancestor   13
Song to a Survivor   14
At Evensong   15
Implicated   16
By Force of Habit, *the keeper of lighthouses*   17
In Your *Ain Toun*   19
From Perth to Edinburgh by Rail   21
Dispatches: From the River   22

Section II: Close to Home

Serendipities	29
Island Songs: A Suite	31
i. *Heart / land*	31
ii. *Of Roots and Wood*	32
iii. *Interruptions*	33
A Way Around Stones	34
Antiphonal Openings	35
Slender Certainties	36
Hushed	38
The Weight of Storms	40
Red-Earth Rites	42
From Dark / To Dove	44
Dance Aweigh	46

Section III: Slippery

Slippery	51
Perhaps	52
Shadow Boxers	54
Along Rosedale Valley Road	56
What is it about flowers	57
Transit Sighting	58
Forest-Dancer	59
The Un-assumed Road	60

Now that I have your heart by heart	61
My mother loved	62
On Tightropes and Tides	63

Section IV: Other Gravities

Senza Titolo	67
On Renderings	68
Tread softly	70
Through the Mouth	71
Discernment	73
Darkly as Through Glass	74
On Syntax and Gestures	75
Palpable Delineations	76
Notes from the Citadel	77
Directions for an Installation	78

Notes	81
Acknowledgements	90

Pinturas ciegas

                                      Even the butterflies
are gone —
            the frosted elfin,
          the Perseus dusky wing,
        trailing the grass-tall prairie.

Wingbeats echo   time's exquisite breathing,
            slender truths
              effaced
      like the silver in old mirrors.

An invitation to pause   before life's blind canvas —
          feel the brushstrokes,
           their silent probing,
       beneath the painting's skin.

I
In the Manner of Tides

"and why we must work to be gentle here"

Dionne Brand, from (XIV ii)
Land to Light On (1997)

Anatomy of Green

I never knew the   moss-green river,
its uneven washes,   subtle bracing.

Rarely touched the sucking ooze   of sand-
fogged bays,   palettes seaweed-streaked.

        Needed to see clearly
    what to step on
or over —
        To sense the underlying
layers,   how pigment
can be diluted —

        Waking each morning
to trace the edges
light to dark.
        Wet,   in the wash.

By Invitation

                        Beyond the windward side
              of islands,   where
       tides dance —   I step
into your silence,

              feel its velvet buoyancy
                    its dark salt anointing
                          the tongue.

                          — Deep ocean's
                  intimate
              undulations,   the teeth
        of reefs —   Your
     wave pools   naked,
   breaking
sweat.

Notes from the Archipelago

1.   Today

a sudden shock of windward rain   beyond the reach of waves.
                    Shadow-fingers sweep
the sand, sculpt the southern shore —
          ocean far as eye can see   sky's naked truth
                    effortless.

The ripe moon rises here   full and sweet above
          the chain of islands:
                    lava cradling the bay   luna-secrets crusted
                              pewter.

2.   *Here, there are revelations*

necessary risks: a slow
                slip-sliding weathering of tides
residue   from a long-melted glacier
    with trails finely marked
              for a soul to follow.

Cadences of solitude and silence
            a scale   tuned to the weight
    of words —   the space
where hyphens open   between
     knowing
          and un-knowing.

3.   Fragments

of memory
                      sinuous as
mist   rest lightly here —

some days they surf
beyond words' tidal reach   tongue
        the waves   play water's skin —
                articulate and intimate

                      always leaving.

Lightning-flashes   bleed
into the wind on *haleakala* —
        house of the sun —   yielding moon-
            scape vistas
                tinted ochre-red.

4.   *A Geography of Voices*

                      Thursday   on the windward side
              rhythms riffle the marsh   their measure
scored in rain-green waves   waxing
      warm against the hills.

                    Night sits
on the lanai   venting
    to the wind
        erasing shores

    the Payne's grey   tongue-tied seas.

5.   *Reefs*

                    tread water   on the sheltered side,
resist undertow,   the churning surf —
                              go nowhere   in particular.

                    Everywhere   this restless dance
of islands,   their simple elegance
        a coral breath deep-held —
                    where even solids   seem to flow,
                            tendered silk.

Maybe

        it is the sea
bearing memory's weight,
    riding nightly
        on the whale's back —

                    Blood-moons
            recall pale clouds,
      autumn's early sigh,   the shiver
of tidepools —

                  maybe this
    is the siren pull   inducing
rivers,   spilling dreams out of
   their mouths.   Remembrance
     buried

          in the deep   drifts quietly
             as light —   and speaks
                   in tongues of fire.

To a Creole Ancestor

                Your traces
linger   in our naked moments,
speak colourless truths   when
the moon is
        new —

                    We are your text,
        your poignant enigmas
reweaving tangled tales —

                    While you lie silent
in shallows   of our green unknowing —
        shedding light.

Song to a Survivor

                You carve
                    textured shadows   in
          the face of stones —
deep petroglyphs   with cambered
        sails,
              your molten rock,   red-orange
                      cooled to black,   rain-forests
                            misting.

Lava's smouldering skin,   the restless paths
        of flow —   like hot wax
                bleeding.

At Evensong

                     stones release
              their secrets —
                               dusk hurls
                         its darkening net
                 into the wind,
           autumnal gesture
         harvesting desire,
winnowing   her long low sustain

as jasmine forests,   rain-fragrant green,
              remember sunlight   blossoms'
                     eloquent weight.

Implicated

> *"what magic words for the getaway"*
> — Olive Senior

Wash your hands before the multitudes,
        declare innocence.

Stay clear of
pharisees and popular demand,
lest   wrongful prisoners be freed.

Like Pilate's wife,
        pay heed   to dreams.

If there are   *magic words,*   they've yet
        to be invoked.
Perhaps   you've toyed with a few —

diaspora

                      redemption

          exile

By Force of Habit,
the keeper of lighthouses

Above the overpass, a flock of starlings
feather-stitch the wind —
it's minus seventeen with wind-chill,
asphalt turning white.

Along Davenport, a pensive statue
benched in bronze,   naked,
alone,
weathers traffic's cold transgressions
steadfast as my great-great grandfather,
Isle of Man lighthouse-keeper,   so they said.

With utmost care
he kept his lamps burning clear,
from sunset to sunrise —
at Chicken Rock, perhaps,   or Dudley Head,
where quiet seas beat
       the cliffs' broken base,
the snow-white surge of surf   honeycombed.

Where each morning
he polished the refractors
to their proper state of brilliancy,
supplied burners with cotton,   lamps with oil —

as light-keeper until the change of watch,
he would remain on guard,   charged
at his peril   to be sober and industrious.

He would make note of
shipwrecks —   record when
the vessel struck the rocks —   careful
        to turn the valves,
keeping the oil-flow,   trimming the wicks,
clean in his person and linens,
admitting no strangers after sunset,
keeping no dogs.

When seas were ebbing, would
he wonder whether, as legends said,
members of St. Bridget's
Nunnery would climb that day
near Horses' Leap —   to sit exposed
on Nun's Chair Rock as penance
        for infractions,   bound
to stay   until the tide twice   ebbed and flowed.

        Or would he contemplate —
revelling in   the turbulent Manx weather,
the breakers' furious rush —
those   rugged cliffs and fierce, contorted
        rocks, basalt weather-worn.

In Your *Ain Toun*

> *The simple things which do not pass*
> *Are shining here*
> — William Soutar

I discovered you
        beyond the river,
its gravelled shallows   home
to herons and moorhens —
red bills tipped   with yellow.

            Stumbled on your *Tay's*   silver steady flow
from wild Southern Highlands towards the firth —
        its tangled gardens
            winding footpaths
                and a railway bridge.

                Explored its edges —
            stone carvings
        among the heather,
caught a kingfisher's   cobalt flash.

I searched archives and registries
conjuring links —   plausible   genealogies.

Compared your profiles
        in weathered portraits —
his   stately, bearded,
            Scottish 1850s-migrant
to a Caribbean isle   yours
poised, clean-shaven,
            1940s poet from Perth.

        Those were the only certainties
in this keen Scottish summer   bracing
as your William Soutar House   near Craigie Hill —
a writer's residence now
           marking your words

enduring as the ageless river
           its plum freshwater pearls.

From Perth to Edinburgh by Rail

          So close
this rush of
brush and brick —
wild trees that bend the wind
        eclipsing sky.

Geldings graze tufts
              of shuffled green
fields   shorn golden.

Low hills   then everywhere
water —
the firth   in slanting sheets of rain
              river's mouth
burnt-umber —
        heaving seas
beyond the cantilevered bridge.

Tonight at dinner
        in twilight's careful
rationing —   a slender   crystal vase
where two carnations   and a solitary rose
        partially
              unfurl.

Dispatches: From the River

i.

        From tree to
tree to tree   a dappled sea of green
floods the ravine —
      birch, alder, ash,
      beech and sycamore —
underfoot   a sheen of
      moss and fern.

        Landscaped
gardens   fringe the woods —
rolling lawns   a moist
viridescence,   freshly mown.

        Everywhere, the constant
cadence of the river —
its copper water's russet flow
among tawny rocks   the colour
of the deer,
      white tails waving.

ii.

                A winding path
steeply silent
        circles the castle
weaves through shadowed brush —
the *Esk's*
        fern and bramble.
Here, there   a buttressed set of stairs
tight against the narrow
                limestone ledge.

                No sieges are likely.
The sandstone-red castle walls
        are deeply thick   impregnable
to all but writers —   their days spent
in nurtured solitude   high
        above the towering rocks.

iii.

                One day, I heard tell
of a heron   sleeping
in a tree —
                encountered deer
in silent contemplation
        unperturbed
as I roamed the castle grounds
and narrow roads   leading
to Rosslyn
            or Bonnyrigg.

              Twice I freed
a *Painted Lady*
wings beating   against the pane —
            fluttering soft
but firm against my palm   they held
        the steadfast quiet beauty
of this place
        its certain grace —

those fragmentary moments
when the sun is freed
from cloud
       when you can read
the trees' translucent heart
and promise of the river —
              its flowing amber light.

II
Close to Home

"as if into an old lake's amber water"

Sue Standing, from "Water Level"
The Cape Split Cycle (1998)

Serendipities

i.

Close to
        home,
even a casual walk
can yield surprises,
chance sightings
        that tug
and probe associations —

green falls of willow tinged
in gold that break
your stride;
flow of leaves beyond the pines'
cascading silence;
        hint of sage
and ash   in morning's
slanted light.

ii.

No wrong moves
for warm drops of sepia
deepening the base
of stalks
        (those unintended
               shadings).

Squeeze
a loaded brush,
something's bound
to fall   between
the russet and   the blue.

All illumination
in the end.
A golden clarity against
        the grain,
revealing the wonderment
              of wet.

Island Songs: A Suite

beginning with Horses in Her Hair: A Granddaughter's Story, *by Rachel Manley*

i.   *Heart / land*

           This tiny
                   consolation
of faith and shelter
       saddled on the wake   of each new swell —
           riding water's back.

                 Its casual
certainty,
brisk salt of
       waking thought —   each day fluid
         as the sea.

              The sun's
careless blessing
is naked and absolute,
       drought skies   unequivocal —
         and then

             it rains
with the conviction
       of ideology —   wild music
           lifting notes.

ii.	*Of Roots and Wood*

     A place where blood
             is lasting —
                       family history
a scent that lingers
and childhood memories
           clump like grass —

squandered dream-lines   etched in faces,
            the silent fear
of seas,   night's blooming cereus,
       its brief
               spectacular hush

mahogany   opening its heart   to let us in —
      movement's quiet tightrope along
the chisel's furrowed track —
      pale glow of
underflesh,
and muscle's slow saunter,
              mirrored   within the grain.

iii.   *Interruptions*

      Beneath all this,
a deeper tide —
                      a restless
            ebullience,
where heat can thicken
      like a kiln on low,
islands too young for
anything but loss to have
            a language —

No space for nuance or margins,
no shades of grey,
just scented frangipani blossoms,
                      and black rocks
      like a sweetness   seeping
           green.

A Way
Around Stones

There are days
when doors open   and light   is liquid —

pools of sky
                reflecting   at your feet.

Weighted days
when consequence   lifts   like February's thaw,

air
        alight   with swallows.

When all is story —
sinew,   bone,   the pulse of narrative.

               Touch   reading tissue
as a text —   laying on   of hands.

The poem's path
breaking lines —   its canvas

       muted blue

Antiphonal Openings

after a painting from the series "Threshold" by Marjorie Moeser

No brashness in this
doorway's arc,
    no burl or twist,   no lines of chatter
angling the grain,
no deviations —   just a seamless, simple
    entrance beckons —   keyless,
      without locks.

    Across the threshold,
a subtle underwash of
    burnt-sienna   inviting
access.
You've been there before —
    this antiphonal space   where
      poetry is —

  where yesterday's silvered joys
and lamentations   call and respond
    as in a psalm.

Slender Certainties

                        Atlantic sun
                 trails morning
         to my window,
strings diamonds
        along the crest
               of a wave —

Sky's clear gaze   discerning
benediction —
a strand
of your hair
        slight   as breath,

touch   of a finger-tip,
skin
of damp trees.

                        Mangrove skipper
                butterflies
        scatter like
snowflakes —
            vining jasmine,
                        buds tinted
pink   in broken sun,
emerald leaves
            the shape of
                        silence —

texture slipping
through the fingers —
            a fine grey sand.

Hushed

for Ariel

   Lightness is easy
in an angel's wake,
       a slender buoyancy
    bereft of shadows.

   Alignment's fleeting moments
        (call them joy).
Still-life mornings
   in redemption's back-lit gaze
     haloed slippery-white.

   Where saints and forests
        tread their faith
on canvas like soft stone —
    absurdities and architecture
   flower, while cloud-song
     pierces cobalt-green.

        Yet even here, emptiness —
                              this subtle in-between
            murmuring:
not yours   not mine   just
                      erosion's sojourn,
      carved citadel besieged,

life's accidental weathering,   to the quick.

The Weight of Storms

Nothing moves
beyond the blue-grey
fences,   cedar-thick with snow,

not the poplar's leafless
etching on
December-leaden sky,

nor the dwarf
Alberta spruce —
time's slow-growth,   silent witness.

No birds at the feeder,
no squirrels   foraging
through lilacs' frozen antlers.

Serene, the season
changes,   proclaims
a take-over,   covers our tracks —

Above the cul-de-sac,
a street lamp's golden orb
sits   like a low-hanging moon.

We play our separate
hands from separate rooms —
lost solitudes —   awaiting ploughs

      to pry us free.

Red-Earth Rites

for Celia

i.

      In these restless hills —
their wild insistence,   Rio Cobre's greening,
sandbank's drift,   the ancient flat bridge,
and crumbling,
      constant gorge.

      In reef-less coastline,
blue-dark,   rugged-steep —
shadowed groves of honeyed palms,   bamboo's
buoyant, skyward surging —
      at Milk River's mouth.

ii.

      We mark her passing —
how one short week ago
she slipped away.
No accompaniment,   no choruses to mask
      her leaving.

No *river running by.*
                    No dirge.

Only dawn's cold indifference —   relentless
           sun rising.

iii.

Her absence cloaked
in hymns and rituals,   the liturgy of grieving.
        Remembering *stars,*   *the rolling thunder,*
God's *terrible swift*
sword —

We take our turns returning her to dust,

                  its stifling closeness
        clay-fired red —
    the weight of heat,
damp and smouldering.

Freed to reap the glories of her morning   unconstrained.

From Dark / To Dove

for Soeur Louise

i.

We sat beside
        the open coffin,
your sister's face,   serene
at last.
White-stone   purified,
        dark to dove.

You asked
where poems come from —
        why for her
life so heavy,   weighted lead,
while all you touched
would blossom   into gold.

ii.

This moment,   I wanted
to say,   is a poem —
        these tears,
probing metaphors,   written
with the heart's   light brush.

            Weighed in
the Halls of Judgment   against
        a feather.

Dance Aweigh

for M. and R.

With every storm,   a story,
chronicled —
seas rising,   then receding —   winds
      at your back.
                               35 knots on the meter,
              spinnaker pole,   a giant sledgehammer.
Anchor dragging / holding,   only the motor
      keeping you   off shoals.

Time to take the satellite view —   Earth
a russet warmth,
turquoise ocean,   flooding
      viridian.

                                  Atlantic waves
            keep coming in —   retracing your course
across the Devil's Backbone,   as you call 'Ole Pot'
      to guide you through.

Once broken skies wax
phthalo-blue,
no hint of dark remaining,   the weathered
      calm will come

                                    beyond the Northern edge —
                  cliffs' narrow gap,   the shallow,
      jagged reefs —   then smooth seas,
            light winds,
                  holding.

III
Slippery

"and she
the stranger I have never met,
only been."

Phoebe Hesketh, from "Stranger"
Netting the Sun (1989)

Slippery

Time's path winds   sinuous
and gravel-fine
through measured days —
        moments
filtered red,   elusive.

Each day   we paddle hard
into the centre
        of the flow —
confront its turbulence,
tones and textures   slate
        to sapphire,
outwashed waves —

chance chroniclers,
wagering   wetly through.

Perhaps

        a day will pass,
or maybe two
before words   slip
like Saturn's probe
        into orbit.

Delicate manoeuvres
on my screen,
        slow and steady,
landscapes randomly revealed.

        An intimate
indifference, the way wind
lifts each kite
equally, ruffles
hair, furrows a lake —
how a shutter slices shadow.

Perhaps this is the way
love stays its
course, hands light on
        the reins.

The way a flame
lingers on
the wick;

intimate in difference.
The way a cat might curl, or a train
        hug the rails.

Shadow Boxers

        Each day
she contemplates the tangled
wood,   a tiny
        Summer Tanager
flies headlong at
the window's bevelled glass,
        wings
splayed   in brick-red
desperation.

        She marvels
at the heft of
banyan roots up-ended,
        sinews
dread-locked,   tightly roped,
the reach
of shadow-boxers.

Invincible
bird veering off
into the densely vine-
wrapped trees.
        Repeating her
relentless quest to
plumb
reflection —   its
inscrutable lustre.

Along Rosedale Valley Road

                the season's lute
                        flat-bellied
                                  fills with rose,
                trills
            maple-red on
wind's unbroken cadence.

                Sunlight gestures
                      long and low
                              across the leaves —
                    a choral symmetry
              in October's golden
        anticipation —
a mellow   double-
    reeded
        O

What is it
about flowers

that petals us
open,   season after season.

First a single
        bract,   then one lone leaf,

then trillium-
like to   bud and bloom in
        vestiges of snow.

Spring's ephemera —
brief as   anemone's passing breeze.

Fresh-leaved
shadows   trace the
        veins of
trees —   crown the lawn.

Soil's seduction,
        squares of
black earth   sprouting green.

From the pond   our wintry
apprehensions   surface   lotus-red.

Transit
Sighting

                                      She prays the rosary
                          from *King* to *Finch,*
                fingering beads —
        stops   *full of grace,*
each decade   measuring
                        the distance —   *Joyful*
              mysteries perhaps,   or *Sorrowful,*
      as travellers   tightly wedged   muffle winter's
                  thick indifference —
compelled to closeness,   the subway's   random offerings.

    Rush-hour's press   against platform walls,   braces
          wind-rush,   train's precursor —
                its tunnelled curve of light
                                evoking rites,
                    and passages —
        swift illumination.

Forest-Dancer

after the painting "Moon over Black Creek" *by Gail Read*

A golden quality to your moon's
        early waxing —
               ochre rhythms
brush-stroked by the creek —   spot-lit
        pirouette of fronds:

              severed sweet
as ripe pineapple —   their measure
        straining free.

A place to sense life's taper,   brace
        the beat —
               discern when to
quicken,   when to pause —   when
        to prune   the dance.

The Un-assumed Road

Memories green this edge of lake,
        thickening reeds,
linger in the mist,
on rain-fresh
summer fern, the subtle willow.

Boulders bear our secrets,
        moss has glossed
the stones,
these clay cliffs rooted
        in memory's axis —
the poignant locus of a curve.

Now only shadows flood the shallows,
trace symmetry's wake
reflecting rain,
        on this the longest day.

Forgetfulness
a tidal flow, shutters of sunlight,
        flash of Prussian blue.

Now that I have your heart by heart

what point remembering —
except to know
that I can summon you by name,
and with each invocation,
the fertile silt of decades.

What good a stirring of the past —
except to fan
untended ashes
best left smouldering.

Too fearful
or perhaps too blind,
I loved   (yet could not see)
perceived the world
through narrow, safer frames,
straddled paths   (explored a few).

Not knowing   truly,
until clamouring years had passed,
how to heed the inclinations
of my heart —
their crimson certainty.

My mother loved

the fragrance of a northern pear,
golden in sweetness,
and now
i'm drawn to
succulent curves,   the jaunty
          leanings of stems

and honeyed textures   grainy   on the tongue

On Tightropes and Tides

        There are hours
as mutable
      as tides
(now you grasp them,
          now you won't)

     moments that linger,
from which there is
         no turning —
their out-wash seared
    encaustic

     Time for observing
small things —
sunlight's inclination,
     angle of a leaf against the pane

work them into lines —
a rope of metaphors
        tightly coiled

Consider gravity,   moments of
              torque —
research winds   and funambulism
    (the risk of falling)
then subtly
    inch your way

IV
Other Gravities

"let no drop spill
between dark and dark."

Phoebe Hesketh, from "Credo"
Netting the Sun (1989)

Senza Titolo

Don't look now,
but I can be undone
by words —
altered
        in the gaze of observations,
                the way certain sightings
can shape a universe,
        a look alone
                split the sky.

As I read the cold
November light
in the company of breakfast
                and dried flowers —

These in-between spaces,   this
                night-before-richness
of a language-to-light-on
relieved of consequence
or absolution.   Just
        melody's hot beauty
                in the throat —

and truth's dark energy   piercing utterly.

On Renderings

i.

Drowning is easy
here —   the poem   dark water,   a falling stone.

No other way
to descend, but   line by line,
lungs filled,   breath packaged,   each word
            weighed   in the palm.

Images turned
over and round   un-threaded lovingly.   Each strand
            catching
      a differently slanted light —

to sieve   and weave this new rendering.

ii.

Rendering anew
this sieve and weave to light,   slanted differently.

Strands caught,
like love un-threaded,   round and over in the palm,
        images weighed.

Each word packaging breath,   filling lungs
        line by line

to descend
no other way,   but stone   falling,
        water dark —

The poem,   where drowning is easy.

Tread softly

        through   a wintered life,
consult lexicographers —   pivot
on meaning's iridescent
          edge.

Sift for significance,   synonyms,
simulacra,   probe
    their many-
          storied layers.
Pan for dreams
among the detritus of spring's
     hard-won melt.

Ponder well   their
    nuanced possibilities
(shimmering lyrical)
    then gently rock them
          free.

Through the Mouth

i.

       Each day we enter labyrinths
            searching
for the centred rose —
the promise
      in its petalled fullness

      no fragrance to entrance us
      no single flush,
      no panicles —

pilgrims,   we take our paths —
swept on,
      minds emptied.

ii.

      Absent   any rules for
          passages
unruly as weather
threading
our way towards
      the haloed edge

     no Icarus wings,   no escape
from our moon-wise
     meanders,   seeking
entrainment   in clouds'
     leadening drift —

        (it's all in the pattern
     they say   a sacred geometry)

the Payne's grey shadows'   fleeting
    symmetries.

Discernment

Always best to heed the fog,
                delay landing,
        re-route —
circle the runway   one more time

        (*Fuel's critical, of course,*   *along with*
             grace: *reserves of*
                energy.)

Pockets of turbulence   preferable to disaster.

    Watch for
                moon-edge
        arcing crisply —
earth's flat circle,   its glowing *limb*.

        (*Beautiful,*   she said of your heart's
            steady beat: *I saved you*
                a picture.)

All crotchets and quavers,   florid syncopations
            echoing.

Darkly as Through Glass

Who can divine
mind's subtle architecture,
predict where stress
will fault a line —
        edges foreshortened,
axes of symmetry awry.

Reason, imploding:
sometime dervish, sometimes
        dark —   a vellum
steeped in doubt.

Unable to read the blueprint of days,
know which beams
        weight-bearing.

This reach of alphabet's
gestures,
its slippery alchemy —   bold
              indifference,
the brilliant
        aligning of stars.

On Syntax and Gestures

                She threads her way
through the chattering crowd,
narrative's thief,
stalking conversations,   clusters of intimacy.

                    [breaking / entering
      a syntax of alignments:
quizzical gaze,   eyebrows raised —
            here and there   gestures
      of recognition]

                Then crisp as sunlight
stitched in snow,   anonymous
as clouds
            she slips away —
a cool indifference
lightly held,   the anchored calm that comes
      with weathering.

Palpable Delineations

Most days our lives withstand,   hold
fast,   unflinching obsidian,   shaped

equally by sunlight,   as inclement
weather.   Then those thick,   unyielding

hours —   boundaries veiled,   landscapes
barely visible   as darkness lowers

her horizon,   and steadfast stone
becomes a house of cards,   jokers tumbling.

This is how you learn to live where fog
blurs —   this liminal space,   everything

stirring —   fissured moonstone,   sand
            and sea,   the lambent air.

Notes from the Citadel

i.

Beams of light
        cross-hatch
the melting night,
its irrevocable
darkness —   trawlers
sit at anchor,
thick   as docks.

ii.

Morning
        gentles
the harbour —
one small sailboat
slicing
opalescent green.

iii.

Later,   a radical
        calm —
shadow's ragged reach
        greys indigo,
strums deep
beneath the slumbering rocks.

iv.

Tomorrow,   the day
will frost,
still as glass —
a swirl of gulls
        slowly circle
our inevitable leaving.

The fog will rise,
as always,
no reversing
one raw glimpse —

clarity's   full throttle.

Directions
for an Installation

Suspend a poem —
        pull taut.

Just enough tension, to ensure
        flex / ibility.

(*And* motion —
        yes,
meaning's not static, after all.)

Hang another,
then another,
        not too close,
yet not too far.

With resonance
        enough for play
          of light —
shadow's
fore / shortening.

A thicket of words   ceiling to floor.

Let readers wander freely
through
the felt sides —

probe type   and watermarks,
touching, turning —
feel them stir.

Even here,
rooted in the gallery,
fibres bond.
Papered words remember
forest floor,   the glorious sting
       of needles.

      Each deckled page
the plumb of
      random leaves,
           unbound.

Notes

Pinturas ciegas
Loosely translated from the Spanish as "blind paintings."

Section I: In the Manner of Tides
The epigraph "and why we must work to be gentle here," is from "XIV ii," by Dionne Brand in *Land to Light On* (Toronto: McClelland & Stewart, 1997, 83).

By Invitation
First published in the anthology *Calling Cards: New Poetry from Caribbean/Canadian Women*, Pamela Mordecai, ed. (Toronto, ON / Kingston, JM: Sandberry Press, 2005, 37).

Notes from the Archipelago
In "2. *Here, there are revelations*," the lines "space/where hyphens open," were suggested by Shyam Selvadurai's comment "my creativity comes not from 'Sri Lankan' or 'Canadian' but precisely from the space between, that marvellous open space represented by the hyphen," in "Questions and Answers, Mr. In-Between," by Liza Cooperman, *National Post*, Saturday, August 28, 2004, RB8.

Maybe
An earlier version of this poem was published in the anthology *Calling Cards: New Poetry from Caribbean/Canadian Women*, Pamela Mordecai, ed. (Toronto, ON / Kingston, JM: Sandberry Press, 2005, 38).

To a Creole Ancestor
The word "creole" is used in the historic sense of "person born in the colonies"/"committed settler," and in reference to the "distinct culture that has evolved in the former plantation societies of the Caribbean." See Olive Senior, *Encyclopedia of Jamaican Heritage* (Twin Guinep Publishers, 2003). An earlier version of the poem was published in the anthology *Calling Cards: New Poetry from Caribbean/Canadian Women*, Pamela Mordecai, ed. (Toronto, ON / Kingston, JM: Sandberry Press, 2005, 35).

Song to a Survivor
The petroglyphs are those in Pu'u Loa, a long low hill of lava in Hawai'i Volcanoes National Park, interpreted by Hawaiians to mean "hill of long life." See *Hawai'i Volcanoes National Park, Fire from Beneath the Sea*, by Barbara and Robert Decker (Mariposa, CA: Sierra Press, 2002, 39). An earlier version of the poem was published in the anthology *Calling Cards: New Poetry from Caribbean/Canadian Women*, Pamela Mordecai, ed. (Toronto, ON / Kingston, JM: Sandberry Press, 2005, 36).

At Evensong
An earlier version of this poem appeared in the anthology *Resonance: Poetry and Art* (Toronto, ON: Sixth Floor Press, 2008) in dialogue with the painting "Adobe Night," acrylic on cloth-covered board, 24" x 18", by Carolyn Jongeward.

Implicated
The epigraph is from the poem "Here and There" by Olive Senior from her collection *Over the Roofs of the World* (London, ON: Insomniac Press, 2005, 57). The references are from the New Testament: Pontius Pilate was the Roman Prefect of Judea who, although he presided over

the trial of Jesus, tried to wash his hands of responsibility for Jesus' death. Pilate's wife, because of a dream, had tried in vain to warn him to have nothing to do with Jesus, "that just man."

By Force of Habit, *the keeper of lighthouses*
Based in part on information and images gleaned from website postings of *Jenkin's Practical Guide to the Isle of Man, 1874,* and the 1874 "Byelaws and Rules and Regulations of the Commissioners of Northern Lighthouses," Chapter III of the *Light-Keepers.*

In Your *Ain Toun*
"Ain toun" is Scots for "own town." The poem's title was suggested by the collection of William Soutar's Scots poems, *My Ain Toun*, published posthumously in 2003 by Perth and Kinross Libraries, Perth. The epigraph is from the poem "June 1943," published in *Into a Room: Selected Poems of William Soutar,* edited and with an introduction by Carl MacDougall and Douglas Gifford, (Perth, Scotland: Argyle Publishing, 2000, 156) and appears by kind permission of The Trustees of the National Library of Scotland. I discovered the poet William Soutar, a revered Scottish writer from Perth (now deceased) while searching the web for information on my Scottish great-grandfather, Simon Soutar. William Soutar's former home now functions as a writer's residence, a tribute to his contributions to Scottish literature. In subsequent trips to Scotland, I have visited the William Soutar House, met with Ajay Close, the then Soutar Fellow/Writer in Residence, and with his niece who lives in Perth. In 2009, I was privileged to read in the main library there at a meeting of the William Soutar House writers' group.

Dispatches: From the River
For the month of September 2009, I was a Fellow at the Hawthornden

International Retreat for Writers in Scotland. The River Esk curves through the steep ravine below the cliff on which Hawthornden Castle is perched. "Dispatches" was written at my desk overlooking the Castle courtyard and the surrounding woods.

Section II: Close to Home
The epigraph "as if into an old lake's amber water" is from "Water Level," for Katherine Kadish by Sue Standing, in *Cape Split Cycle* (1998), Katherine Kadish, monotypes, Sue Standing, poems. Exhibition catalogue, Virginia Museum of Fine Arts, included with permission of the author.

Island Songs: A Suite
"Island Songs" is a variation on a found poem, building on words and phrases culled from the memoir *Horses in Her Hair: A Granddaughter's Story* by Rachel Manley, (Toronto, ON: Key Porter Books, 2008) and included with permission of the author.

A Way Around Stones
The title was suggested by the sentence "Water finding its way around stones" from the poem "Bee and Woman: An Anatomy" in *Quick* by Anne Simpson (Toronto, ON: McClelland & Stewart, 2007, 56). Thanks to Dr. Paula Nieuwstraten for a brief conversation about the importance of attention to story and the laying on of hands. An earlier version of this poem first appeared in the anthology *Resonance: Poetry and Art* (Toronto, ON: Sixth Floor Press, 2008), in dialogue with the painting "Shape #2 (blue), watercolour and gauze, 10" x 14", by Barbara Feith.

Antiphonal Openings
The following references are taken from the terminology of doors:

brashness (a condition characterized by a low resistance to shock and abrupt failure across the grain); *burl* (a twist or swirl in the grain of wood, which usually occurs near a knot but does not contain a knot); *chatter* (lines that appear across a door at right angles to the grain); a *deviation* (a twist or deviation in which one or more corners of a door are out of plane with the other corners). Source: Web *Door Terms Encyclopedia*. An earlier version of this poem appeared in the anthology *Resonance: Poetry and Art* (Toronto, ON: Sixth Floor Press, 2008, 49), in response to a painting from the series, "Threshold," oil stick on canvas, 18" x 24", by Marjorie Moeser.

Slender Certainties

Image in lines 13-14 suggested by "His skin reminds her of damp trees, a forest alive" from *Spirit of Haiti* by Myriam Chancy, (London: Mango Publishing, 2003, 8). The poem first appeared in the anthology *Resonance: Poetry and Art* (Toronto, ON: Sixth Floor Press, 2008) in dialogue with the painting "Low Tide," watercolour, 30" x 38", by Barbara Andersen.

Hushed

Poem influenced by a visit to the exhibit "*Sin and Salvation: Holman Hunt and the Pre Raphaelite Vision*" (Toronto: Art Gallery of Ontario, Spring 2009).

Red-Earth Rites

Reference to "river running by" is taken from "All Things Bright and Beautiful" by Cecil F. Alexander (1848), the entrance hymn from the Mass of Thanksgiving for the life of my cousin, Celia J. Kennedy (September 19, 1942 – October 12, 2008). The reference to "stars … the rolling thunder" is taken from the recessional hymn "How Great Thou

Art" by Carl G. Boberg. The reference to God's "terrible swift sword" is from "Mine Eyes Have Seen the Glory" by Julia Ward Howe (1816).

From Dark / To Dove
Stanza i: In alchemy, lead symbolizes, among other things, the sinner's soul. It is also depicted as containing a dove, indicative of its ability to release the spirit after death and purification.

Stanza ii: In ancient Egypt, the heart was believed to contain the mind and soul. It was believed to be weighed after death against a feather in the Halls of Judgment (Rowena & Rupert Shepherd, *1,000 Symbols*. London: Thames and Hudson, 2002, 47, 49, 157).

An earlier version of the poem appeared in the chapbook anthology *The Long Dash* (Toronto, ON: Sixth Floor Press, 2005, 21–22).

Dance Aweigh
This poem is for my sister and brother-in-law. It incorporates elements from their ham radio e-mails as they sailed the waters of the Atlantic through the Outport Islands of the Bahamas. *Dance Aweigh* is their 1982 Endeavour 40 sloop; 'Ole Pot' is the pilot whose ancestors were shipwrecked on Devil's Backbone in the 1600s.

Section III: Slippery
The epigraph "and she/ the stranger I have never met,/ only been" is from "Stranger" by Phoebe Hesketh in *Netting the Sun: New and Collected Works*, with an introduction by Anne Stevenson, Limited edition: 151/200 (London: Enitharmon Press, 1989, 126), and is included with appreciation to Enitharmon Press/the Literary Estate of Phoebe Hesketh.

What is it about flowers
An earlier version of this poem was published in *Garden Variety, An Anthology of Flower Poems,* Lily Contento, ed. (Thornhill, ON: Quattro Books, 2007, 73).

Transit Sighting
The "rosary" refers to both the beads that Roman Catholics use to count prayers and to the meditative prayer that contemplates four sets of mysteries in the life of Christ and his mother, the Blessed Virgin Mary. Each mystery of the rosary (Joyful, Sorrowful, Glorious, and Luminous) consists of five decades, that is, ten beads per decade. The *Hail Mary* is the central prayer of the rosary and is counted on the beads. The italicized phrase *"full of grace"* is taken from the first line of the prayer. An earlier version of the poem was published in the anthology *Calling Cards: New Poetry from Caribbean/Canadian Women,* Pamela Mordecai, ed. (Toronto, ON / Kingston, JM: Sandberry Press, 2005, 83).

Forest-Dancer
Thanks to Gail Read for her painting "Moon over Black Creek," watercolour on paper, 22" x 30".

The Un-assumed Road
An "un-assumed road" is one that has been constructed, but not yet assumed for maintenance by a township. It is usually flagged by a sign indicating "Un-assumed Road. Use at your own risk." See *Township of Hamilton, By-Law No. 2008-26,* 1. i.

Now that I have your heart by heart
The poem was triggered by the beginning of the last line of Louise

Bogan's 1949 poem "Song for the Last Act" reprinted by permission of Mary Kinzie, literary executor for the Estate of Louise Bogan.

Section IV: Other Gravities
The epigraph "let no drop spill / between dark and dark" is from "Credo" by Phoebe Hesketh in *Netting the Sun: New and Collected Poems,* with an introduction by Anne Stevenson, Enitharmon Press, Limited edition: 151/200 (London: Enitharmon Press, 1989, 179). Included with appreciation to Enitharmon Press/the Literary Estate of Phoebe Hesketh.

Senza Titolo
This Italian phrase means "Untitled." The poem plays with notions from quantum physics and the uncertainty principle. The phrase "a language-to-light-on" is a riff on the title of Dionne Brand's poetry collection *Land to Light On.* The poem, along with its back story, first appeared in the *Poet to Poet* anthology, Julie Roorda and Elana Wolff, eds. (Toronto: Guernica Editions, 2012, p. 72).

On Renderings
A variation on a palindrome reflecting on the experience of rendering into English three poems by a Spanish-speaking poet. The poem first appeared in *Poetry Wales*, Spring 2012, Volume 47, Number 4, p. 21.

Through the Mouth
Information on labyrinths, patterns, and sacred geometry are from the website of the Labyrinth Society <www.labyrinthsociety.org>. An earlier version of this poem entitled "on thresholds" appeared in the anthology *Resonance: Poetry and Art* (Toronto, ON: Sixth Floor Press, 2008), in dialogue with the painting from the series "Threshold,"

acrylic on cloth-covered board, 18" x 24", by Marjorie Moeser.

Discernment
When viewed from the side, Earth looks like a flat circle, and the atmosphere appears like a halo around it. This glowing halo is known as the limb. Thanks to NASA's "Notes on a Barren Moon," August 8, 2001. A *crotchet* is a quarter note in music; a *quaver* is an eighth note.

Darkly as Through Glass
Vellum is the paper on which architectural drawings are currently made. Originally a "parchment paper made from the skin of calves prepared for writing or printing by long exposure in a bath of lime and by repeated rubbings with a burnisher; also the skin of goats or kids prepared in a similar manner." Source: *A Complete Dictionary of Dry Goods* by George S. Cole, W.B. Conkey Company, Chicago, Printers and Binders, 1892.

Notes from the Citadel
Written on the occasion of the League of Canadian Poets' Annual General Meeting, held for the first time in St. John's, Newfoundland and Labrador, June 2008.

Directions for an Installation
The *felt* side of the paper is the best side for printing. The *deckle* is a wooden frame that leaves the edges of the paper slightly irregular and wavy. Deckle edges are one of the indicators that the paper was made by hand. Source: *The Properties of Paper*, 2003, Ballarpur Industries Ltd. <www.bitpaper.com/atoz2.asp#15>.

Acknowledgements

Special thanks to Luciana Ricciutelli, Editor-in-Chief, Inanna Publications, for her belief in my work and all that goes into producing a beautiful book.

Thanks to Allan Briesmaster for his thoughtful editing; Rachel Manley, Olive Senior, and Rosemary Blake for their helpful reading of the manuscript; John Oughton for his evocative cover photograph; Jean L. Stinson for her meticulous copyediting/proofing and supportive friendship; Clara Blackwood, John Oughton, Merle Nudelman, Sheila Stewart, Elana Wolff, and Rosemary Blake, writing friends from the Long Dash group; Ajay Close, William Soutar Fellow/Writer-in-residence during my visits to Perth, Scotland. And to Anne-Marie Caron-Réaume, my thanks always, for her caring presence.

The trajectories of several poems were influenced/inspired by the work of artists Marjorie Moeser, Barbara Feith, Carolyn Jongeward, Barbara Andersen and Gail Read. Appreciation also to artists Mary Lou Payzant, Wendy Weaver, Lynne Ritchie, and Beryl Goering. All were initial members of the collaborative project between Studio Artists from the Women's Art Association of Canada and the Long Dash group of poets.

Thanks to the editors of the following publications where several of the poems first appeared, some in earlier incarnations: *Poetry Wales; Calling Cards: New Poetry from Jamaican/Canadian Women; Garden Variety: An Anthology of Flower Poems;* and the *Poet to Poet* anthology.

For the creative space to work on the manuscript of *Dark Water Songs*, my enduring appreciation to the Hawthornden International Retreat for Writers in Lasswade, Scotland, where I was a Fellow in September, 2009.

Photo: Sue MacLeod.

Mary Lou Soutar-Hynes, is a Jamaican-Canadian, poet/educator and former nun with an interest in poetic inquiry. A 2009 Hawthornden Fellow, her publications include the collections: *Travelling Light* (2006), long-listed for the 2007 ReLit Poetry Award, and *The Fires of Naming* (2001). Her poetry and essays have appeared in journals such *Canadian Woman Studies/ les cahiers de la femme*, *Poetry Wales* and *Quills*, and in the anthologies/ publications *Calling Cards: New Poetry from Caribbean/Canadian Women* (2005); *Resonance: Poetry and Art* (2008); *The Art of Poetic Inquiry* (2012); *Jamaica in the Canadian Experience: A Multiculturalizing Presence* (2012); *Jubilation! Poems Celebrating 50 Years of Jamaican Independence* (2012); and in *Poet to Poet* (2012). She has lived in Toronto since her arrival in 1969.